Energy at Work

by Mary Beth Spann

PEARSON

Glenview, Illinois
Boston, Massachusetts
Chandler, Arizona
Upper Saddle River, New Jersey

Photographs

Every effort has been made to secure permission and provide appropriate credit for photographic material. The publisher deeply regrets any omission and pledges to correct errors called to its attention in subsequent editions.

Unless otherwise acknowledged, all photographs are the copyright © of Dorling Kindersley, a division of Pearson.

Photo locators denoted as follows: Top (T), Center (C), Bottom (B), Left (L), Right (R), Background (Bkgd)

Opener: ©Royalty-Free/Corbis; FP3 (B) Getty Images; FP5 (BR) ©Charles E. Rotkin/Corbis, (TR, TL, BL) Getty Images; 4 Image Source/Getty Images; 6 (Inset) Getty Images, (Bkgd) Getty Images; 8 Courtesy of the London Toy and Model Museum, Paddington, London/©DK Images; 9 Getty Images; 10 (Bkgd) Getty Images; 11 (Inset) The Image Works, Inc.; 13 ©DK Images, (Inset) ©Charles E. Rotkin/Corbis; 14 Getty Images; 15 ©Reuters/Corbis; 18 (Inset) Kindra Clineff/Index Stock Imagery, (Bkgd) Getty Images; 19 ©Royalty-Free/Corbis.

ISBN-13: 978-0-328-61790-6
ISBN-10: 0-328-61790-3

6 7 8 9 10 V0FL 16 15 14 13

What You Already Know

Energy, the ability to do work, comes in many different forms. Your body works constantly. As it works, you use energy.

Energy comes in many forms. Light, heat, and sound are forms of energy. So too is electrical energy.

Stored energy is energy that can be used later. Energy of motion is the energy carried by moving objects. Different forms of stored energy can change into different forms of energy in motion. A compression wave is a sound wave that moves when air particles are pressed together and then spread apart.

These bicyclists are changing the stored energy in their muscles to energy of motion.

Friction is the rubbing of one object against another. It changes energy of motion into heat energy.

The following book describes the many ways that we capture, store, and use energy. People in states such as California use new technologies to capture and store energy. These new technologies might help us cut down on pollution and produce more energy on our own. Keep reading to find out about capturing and storing energy!

When you rub your hands together, you produce friction.

Types of Energy

Stored energy is also called potential energy. Energy that causes change is also known as kinetic energy.

Potential energy is energy of position or state. Objects that can fall have potential energy. Objects that are squeezed or stretched have potential energy.

An object's kinetic energy depends on its weight and speed. Objects are constantly shifting between their kinetic and potential energy, based on whether they are at rest or in motion.

All of the kinetic and potential energy that we use comes from resources in the environment. These resources can be renewable or nonrenewable.

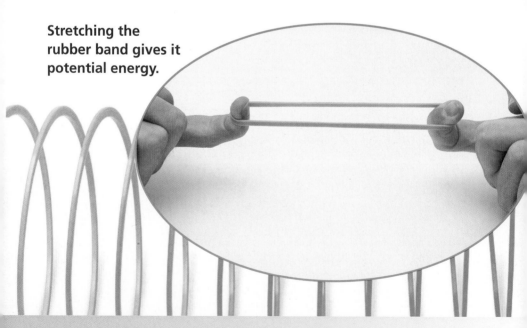

Stretching the rubber band gives it potential energy.

Nonrenewable Energy

Nonrenewable energy resources cannot be replaced once they are used up. We are using them up quickly. The United States has gone from being able to supply its own oil to having to import 12 million barrels a day.

Our use of nonrenewable energy resources has created a lot of pollution. But compared to the cost of renewable resources, they have been much cheaper.

The most important nonrenewable energy resources are the fossil fuels. Fossil fuel forms from the remains of dead animals and plants. The major fossil fuels are oil, coal, and natural gas. These three nonrenewable energy resources are used to make nearly nine-tenths of the energy used in the United States each year.

Oil (left), coal (center), and natural gas (right) are the most important nonrenewable energy resources.

Coal

Humans have been using coal for energy longer than any other fossil fuel. The steam-powered ships, railroads, and factories of the Industrial Revolution were powered by coal. Coal was first used to make electricity in the late 1800s. Over the past century, more and more coal has been used to make electricity. Its use in other industries has stayed about the same.

In the year 2003, slightly over half of all the electricity produced in the United States was made from coal. Coal is also used to make products such as steel, cement, and paper. In the United States, coal is mined primarily in southeastern states such as West Virginia and Kentucky and western states such as Wyoming.

Energy from coal is used to make many products, such as the paper shown here.

The U.S. Department of Energy expects worldwide coal use to increase by one-third in the near future. At the same time, western Europe is expected to shift much of its coal use to natural gas use. But China and India's increased coal use will most likely make up for the changes in western Europe. These fast-growing Asian countries are expected to make up two-thirds of the rise in coal use over the next thirty years.

The burning of coal usually causes a lot of pollution. But now there is technology that allows people to burn coal in a way that causes less pollution. This technology removes harmful substances such as sulfur and nitrogen from coal. It also cut downs on the amount of carbon dioxide released by coal burning.

Coal mines (below) move around tons of earth while mining coal (right), which contains sulfur and nitrogen.

Oil

The United States got about two-fifths of its energy from oil in 2004. We used nearly as much energy from oil that year as from coal and natural gas combined. We used 20 million barrels of oil a day in 2004.

The United States' demand for oil has gone up faster than we can pump it from the ground. More than half of the oil we use now is from other countries.

Higher oil prices have allowed oil companies to find ways of getting more oil out of the ground. One way, called "waterflooding," pumps water into rock. The water pushes the oil up to the surface. Other methods use steam and carbon dioxide to force oil out of the ground.

Oil refineries change oil to gasoline. We use gasoline to run our cars, trucks, and planes. Oil heats our homes and offices. It is also used to make medicines, plastics, ink, crayons, bubble gum, dishwashing liquids, deodorant, eyeglasses, records, tires, ammonia, and heart valves.

This toy robot's plastic parts were produced from oil.

Oil products make our life easier. But finding, making, moving, and using oil causes air and water pollution. Exploring and drilling for oil can damage land and ocean habitats. The burning of oil causes air pollution. Oil that is spilled into rivers or oceans can harm wildlife. The use of oil will increase over the next several decades. So it is important that humans find a way to make oil use friendlier for the environment.

This offshore oil rig draws oil up from the sea floor.

Natural Gas

Over time, pressure and heat have changed some plant and animal remains into methane gas. Methane gas, which has no color or smell, makes up natural gas.

Natural gas is moved from natural gas fields by pipelines. These pipelines ship natural gas all over the United States. If natural gas is chilled to -162°C (-260°F), it becomes a liquid. The liquid natural gas can then be stored or shipped in large ships called tankers.

Around the time of World War II, the United States began building a nationwide natural gas pipeline. It gave a big boost to natural gas use. In 2003, almost 62 million American homes used natural gas in things such as stoves, furnaces, water heaters, and clothes dryers.

These tanks store natural gas, which is used in many homes' stoves to cook food.

Natural gas has advantages as a fuel source. It creates little pollution compared to oil and coal. It is easy to burn, and burns efficiently, with little waste left over. Natural gas can be moved easily from one place to another through pipelines.

Natural gas also has disadvantages. Natural gas plants are at risk from storms. When Hurricanes Katrina and Rita hit the United States in 2005, they badly damaged natural gas plants. And it is becoming harder to pump natural gas from the ground. Natural gas companies are exploring newer and better ways for obtaining natural gas. One way creates fractures, or small holes, in underground rocks where natural gas is located. The fractures help the gas escape more easily.

This public bus runs on natural gas, which pollutes less than gasoline.

Renewable Energy

Renewable energy resources are not unlimited. But they can be naturally replaced in a fairly short time. We use energy from the Sun's heat, the flow of river water, and the breakdown of plant and animal remains to create renewable energy resources. Right now renewable energy resources are being used up much less than nonrenewable sources of energy.

Compared to nonrenewable sources of energy, the use of most renewable energy resources causes less harm to the environment. Their use also causes less pollution. The more we use renewable energy resources, the less threat there is of energy sources overall being used up.

Solar cells, wind turbines, and hydroelectric dams each use a different renewable energy resource to make electricity.

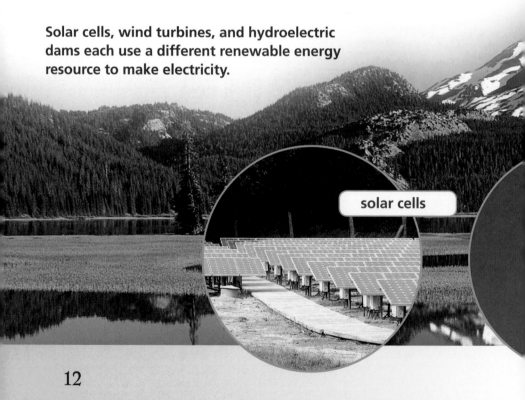

solar cells

Renewable energy resources make up less than one-tenth of the energy used in the United States each year. One reason they are used so little is that they are still too expensive as a fuel source. For example, the cost of making electricity from wind power has dropped by nearly nine-tenths over the past 30 years, from 40 cents a kilowatt-hour to 5 cents a kilowatt-hour. Even so, it is still about four times more costly to make electricity from wind power than from natural gas.

The following pages discuss three important renewable energy resources: solar power, wind power, and hydropower. Each has benefits when compared to nonrenewable sources of energy. But each also has major drawbacks.

wind turbines

hydroelectric dam

Solar Power

Solar power is energy we gather from the Sun. The Sun has been making energy for billions of years. Its light contains a massive amount of energy. The amount of sunlight received by the United States each day equals about two times the energy we use each year!

Despite the energy available from sunlight, solar power makes up just one-tenth of 1 percent of the energy we use each year. The cost of making electricity from one type of solar power has dropped by four-fifths over the past 20 years. But the equipment used to collect solar energy takes up lots of space and contains toxic substances. Such drawbacks have stopped people from using more solar power.

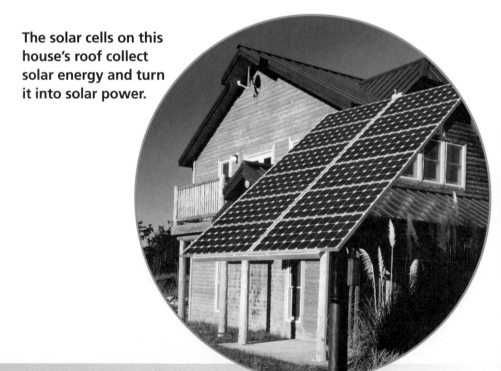

The solar cells on this house's roof collect solar energy and turn it into solar power.

One way we capture solar power is through passive solar heating. This is when sunlight shines through a window and heats a building, or when sunlight falls on the water in a swimming pool and heats it.

Another process uses photovoltaic, or solar cell, systems. These systems are made from material that can conduct electricity and absorb sunlight. When sunlight hits the system, the energy from the light excites the system's cells. Parts within the cells split off and flow across the cells. This generates electricity.

In larger solar power plants, sunlight is absorbed by rows and rows of curved troughs. These troughs are filled with a special oil that heats up. The heated oil heats water to make steam. The steam turns a turbine, which powers a generator that makes electricity.

These solar cars get their energy from sunlight.

Wind Power

Wind power is energy we capture from the wind. The Sun's uneven heating of Earth forms areas of high pressure and low pressure in the air. Wind flows between them to even out the difference in pressure. As long as Earth gets sunlight, there will be wind!

Wind power and solar power are tied together in other ways. As with solar energy, there is a huge amount of wind energy waiting to be captured in states such as California. As you already know, the price of producing electricity from each has dropped by a lot in recent years. Still, wind energy, like solar energy, makes up only a tiny fraction of the energy we use each year. However, our ability to produce power from wind has increased substantially in the past several years.

Wind farms made up of hundreds of wind turbines are found in several places in California.

For centuries, people have used windmills to capture wind energy. Windmills helped farmers pump water, grind wheat, and cut wood. As late as the 1940s, Americans in rural areas used them to make electricity.

Now, wind turbines are used to create electricity from the wind. These turbines are made up of blades mounted on a rotor. The turbines are placed on top of towers that reach 100 feet into the air. At that height the wind flows stronger and more smoothly.

As the wind blows, low-pressure pockets of air form on the side of the blade that is not being hit by the wind. The pressure makes the blade spin. The spinning blade turns the rotor, which then turns a shaft. And the shaft spins a generator that makes electricity.

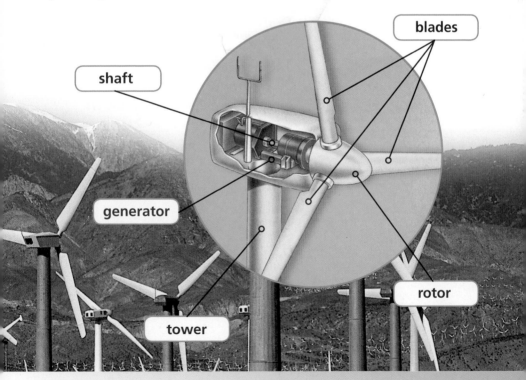

blades

shaft

generator

rotor

tower

Hydropower

Hydropower is energy we capture from flowing water. Hydropower was first used to turn water wheels to grind grain, and to move paddleboats.

In 2003, hydropower supplied almost 3 percent of the energy consumed in the United States. This energy, in the form of electricity, made up almost one-tenth of the electricity used in the United States in 2003. At the time hydropower also accounted for around three-quarters of all energy produced from renewable resources.

Hydroelectricity is created by hydroelectric dams that block huge rivers. Behind the dams are reservoirs of water. The water flows through the dams' turbines. It pushes against the blades of the turbines. This causes the turbines to spin generators that make electricity.

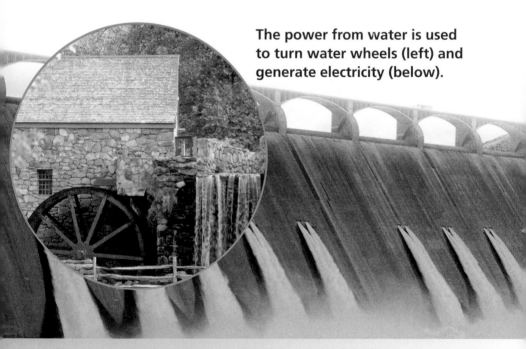

The power from water is used to turn water wheels (left) and generate electricity (below).

Making hydroelectricity pollutes the air and water less than the burning of fossil fuels. Hydroelectricity is also very cheap. But hydroelectric dams block animals from swimming upstream and downstream. These dams change the water temperature and the current. They also flood the land, which can damage habitats. As a result, few hydroelectric dams have been built recently, and some people want older dams destroyed.

Humans have developed many ways to capture and store energy from renewable resources. But until energy from renewable resources becomes as cheap as energy from oil, coal, and natural gas, we are stuck with fossil fuels as our main source of power. Maybe you will find a way to get cheap energy from renewable resources!

The energy from this waterfall can create massive amounts of electricity.

Glossary

fossil fuel　　　　　　a fuel formed from the remains of living things

hydroelectricity　　　electricity produced through the power of moving water

kilowatt-hour　　　　a unit of electrical energy equal to a thousand watts in one hour

methane　　　　　　　a colorless, odorless, flammable gas that makes up natural gas

nonrenewable resource　　a source of energy that cannot be replaced once it is used up

renewable resource　　a source of energy that can be replaced in a fairly short time

turbine　　　　　　　an engine containing blades that are rotated by water, steam, or air pressure

waterflooding　　　　a method of removing oil by flooding oil-containing rocks with water